to Karen and Bob
From San Fran to Sante Fe
to Del Ray Beach.
Cheers!
Cynthie Lee Ketover

The Cocktail Chronicles

with recipes

Cynthia Lee Katona

Published by White Mule Press,
a division of the American Distilling Institute™.

© 2014 Cynthia Lee Katona
photomerchant.com

Printed in the United States of America.

ISBN 978-0-9910436-4-4

whitemulepress.com
cheers@whitemulepress.com

PO Box 577
Hayward, CA 94541

Recipes

INTRODUCTION

This book might be the story of my life as seen through the lens of a cocktail glass. Or it might be a cocktail glass as seen through the lens of my life. It could be a travelogue, or a testament to the fact that most accidents, and most miracles, happen within twenty miles of home. It could easily have been entitled *Zen and the Art of Cocktail Preparation*, or *Much Ado about Bitters*. It is probably the only booze book ever written that is organized chronologically. To quote that old country sage Tanya Tucker, "it might be more than you're after, or not nearly enough." Whatever it is — *Salute!*

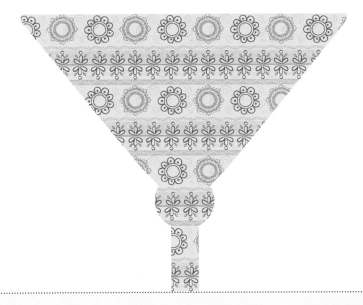

V
O
L
P
O
L
I
C
E
L
L
A

THIS LIGHT, FRAGRANT TABLE WINE, PRODUCED IN THE NOUVEAU STYLE IS A NATURAL SEDATIVE FOR THE PRE-TODDLING SET.

My father was a first generation American, smuggled into the United States in the painfully distended belly of a young Sicilian woman from *Castellammare del Golfo*, a fortress town just outside of Palermo. My father's later involvement with Al Capone and the mafia and ultimately the United States Witness Protection Program make the accurate naming of my grandparents impossible, but on my birth certificate my father shows up as Jerry Joseph Nevarre, dancer. While my father was rather a good dancer, it was not actually his occupation. This was my mother's habitual way of taking him to task for being a gambler and a bit of a gigolo. She enjoyed creating alternate identities for him: he shows up on my communion records as a *masseur*, and later on my confirmation application as a *maitre'd*. Had he been present at these iconic events, I suppose he might have been able to defend himself. ■ While Jerry Joseph Nevarre could not be called a good husband, he was the most remarkable and magical father. Think Roberto Benigni in *Life is Beautiful* crossed with Don Corleone. Everything was a game to him, and somehow he had the power to make anything happen. He was a "house husband" and a "mr. mom" forty years before those terms were invented, and his fathering techniques were both old school and unconventional. ■ One of the results of this was that I had my first drink when I was still in swaddling. While I don't really remember my first Valpolicella and Water, I do remember subsequent drams, as my father insisted on bottle feeding me until I was nearly three. This light, fragrant table wine, produced in the nouveau style is a natural sedative for the pre-toddling set. Chianti Classico and Barolo work equally as well.

VOLPOLICELLA & WATER

3/4 BABY BOTTLE OF TAP WATER
1/4 BABY BOTTLE OF GOOD ITALIAN RED WINE
SHAKE WELL AND SERVE AT ROOM TEMPERATURE
TO AVOID BURPING.

MY FATHER AND I DROVE FROM OUR APARTMENT IN THE SLUMS OF HOLLYWOOD TO CHASEN'S IN BEVERLY HILLS, THE RESTAURANT CREDITED WITH HAVING INVENTED A COCKTAIL IN 1939 FOR SHIRLEY TEMPLE ON THE EVENT OF HER TENTH BIRTHDAY.

In 1954 my mother, spiffy and highly professional, with her fancy handkerchief arrangement pinned neatly to her chest, was a waitress at Du-Pars, the well known restaurant and bakery in the famous Farmers Market in West Hollywood. My father was still apparently just a "dancer," a "*masseur*," or a "chauffeur," depending on my mother's opinion of him at the time. ■ I had just turned seven, and the Catholic Church decided that I had reached the age of reason and responsibility simultaneously with my father's decision that I should start ordering my own drinks when we went out for dinner. ■ As my mother toiled for tips from NBC junior executives, and cops who were encouraged by the Du-Pars' management to stop by for free coffee, my father and I drove from our apartment in the slums of Hollywood to Chasen's in Beverly Hills, the restaurant credited with having invented a cocktail in 1939 for Shirley Temple on the event of her tenth birthday. ■ Dressed like it was Easter Sunday, and well coached, I knew just what to say when my father told the waiter he would like a "Dewar's on the rocks," and then asked me what I would like to drink. "I'll have a Shirley Temple, with an extra cherry please."

SHIRLEY TEMPLE

INGREDIENTS
3 OZ LEMON-LIME SODA
3 OZS GINGER ALE
DASH GRENADINE
MARASCHINO CHERRY FOR GARNISH
PREPARATION
POUR THE LEMON-LIME SODA AND GINGER ALE INTO A COLLINS GLASS WITH ICE CUBES. ADD A DASH OF GRENADINE. STIR. GARNISH WITH A CHERRY.

MY FATHER, IN A BLACK SHIRT AND TIE AND A BEAUTIFUL
ARMANI SUIT, DRESSED ME LIKE A LITTLE COWBOY,
COMPLETE WITH HOLSTER AND SIX SHOOTERS, AND
DROVE INTO THE DESERT TO MEET SEVEN SEVERE LOOKING
MEN, WHOSE SUITS WERE CLEARLY NOT BESPOKE.

In 1955, my father, in a black shirt and tie and a beautiful Armani suit, dressed me like a little cowboy, complete with holster and six shooters, and drove into the desert to meet seven severe looking men, whose suits were clearly not bespoke. The meeting took place at a ranch in Hesperia owned by Roy Rogers, and quite frankly once we arrived, I felt like I was the only one who had come appropriately dressed. ■ My father got out of the car and immediately handed me over to Dale Evans, before joining the other men in a room that felt preternaturally hushed and sepulchral. Dale deftly steered me towards the paddock, and Bullet was there, and

Trigger, and I was put on a pony and encouraged to ride in a large circle for nearly an hour, while who knows what was going on inside? ■ I never saw Roy Rogers, who was a notorious teetotaler, and I was not offered a drink while I was there, but from that day on I never ordered another Shirley Temple. I was strictly a Roy Rogers kinda girl.

ROY ROGERS

INGREDIENTS

1/4 OZ GRENADINE

COLA

MARASCHINO CHERRY FOR GARNISH

PREPARATION

POUR THE INGREDIENTS INTO A COLLINS GLASS FILLED WITH ICE. STIR WELL. GARNISH WITH THE MARASCHINO CHERRY.

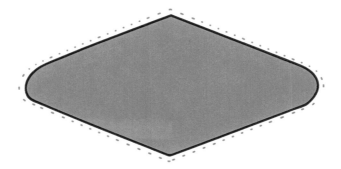

It was 1957. I was almost ten and the Sands in Vegas had already been open for four years and gained a reputation as the coolest casino on the fledgling strip. My father was as habitual a guest there as Frank Sinatra and the rest of the Rat Pack. Our custom was to play blackjack with pennies in our room late into the evening at the adjacent Desert Inn until he felt "hot," and then he would hit the tables in earnest. I would usually fall asleep almost as soon as he left for the Sands, hoping that he would win, and come back for me so that we could watch the evening show at the Copa Room. Nowadays, casinos are overrun with families and screaming children, but back then they were serious, adult places. The men wore elegant suits and the women were glamorous. I never saw another child my age. While I must have seen many famous stars

SICILIANS BELIEVE THAT IT IS BAD LUCK TO TOAST WITH
WATER, SO WHEN MY FATHER PROPOSED A TOAST THAT NIGHT,
HE POURED A BIT OF HIS RUSTY NAIL INTO MY GLASS.

perform there, the person I really remember was Antonio Morelli, the charming casino band leader, because he was there all the time and he would always stop by and say hello to my father after his last set. ■ Sicilians believe that it is bad luck to toast with water, so when my father proposed a toast that night, he poured a bit of his rusty nail into my glass. We clinked rims, and he said, "Always remember that I love you." I did not know the rusty nail that night would be the last drink we would have together. I did not know then that magical fathers often disappear.

RUSTY NAIL

INGREDIENTS
1 1/2 OZ SCOTCH WHISKY
1/2 OZ DRAMBUIE
1 TWIST LEMON PEEL

PREPARATION
POUR THE SCOTCH AND DRAMBUIE INTO AN OLD-FASHIONED GLASS ALMOST FILLED WITH ICE CUBES. STIR WELL. GARNISH WITH THE LEMON TWIST.

MY UNCLE EDDIE WAS A BIT OF AN *AFICIONADO*. ONLY MOONSHINE FROM THE STILLS OF RABUN COUNTY COULD SATISFY HIS TASTE...

After my father vanished, my life changed dramatically. I was no longer daddy's little princess. My mother returned to the bosom of her own redneck, fundamentalist, Germanic family, and I was the only Catholic, black-haired, brown- eyed, peculiarly sophisticated kid they had ever met. ■ It was the late '50's and my loud and rowdy uncles did not sip cocktails in plush red leather booths or tip lavishly. They wore buffalo plaid shirts, ate at Bob's Big Boy, nursed coffees in corner diners, and left stray pennies for the waitresses who routinely put up with their crude compliments. ■ What they did do though was introduce me to Georgia moonshine... the real deal. My uncle Eddie was a bit of an *aficionado*. Only moonshine from the stills of Rabun County could satisfy his taste, so late on a Thursday night, he would call in sick to his gas station in Glendale and hit the road for the 2,500 mile journey to the mountains of Georgia, where the moonlight obscured the illegal activities of his favorite stills. On Monday night he would arrive back home with a trunk full of mason jars — some for sale to defray the costs of the trip — some for us. ■ Never having been excluded from any drinking activity, I naturally asked uncle Eddie for my own shot of white lightening. He thought it was cute until he realized that I could drink him under the table. I have loved hard liquor ever since.

GEORGIA MOONSHINE

ILLEGAL MOONSHINE IS STILL THE BEST, BUT IF YOU DON'T HAVE AN UNCLE EDDIE, YOU CAN GET GEORGIA MOON CORN WHISKEY (80 PROOF), JUNIOR JOHNSON MIDNIGHT MOON APPLE PIE MOONSHINE (70 PROOF), AND MIDNIGHT MOON JUNIOR JOHNSON STRAWBERRY MOONSHINE (100 PROOF) AT: WWW.MARKETVIEWLIQUOR.COM/ PRODUCT/GEORGIA-MOON-CORN-WHISKEY-BOURBON-750ML.HTML

OUR NEWLY CONSTRUCTED FAMILY DID WHAT THE FOLKS
IN AA CALL "DOING A GEOGRAPHIC," MOVING NORTH FOUR
HUNDRED MILES TO CASTRO VALLEY TO PRETEND THAT WE HAD
ALWAYS BEEN AN ORDINARY, INTACT, NUCLEAR FAMILY.

In 1961 my mother remarried. The hell-raising uncles were once again banished, because my new stepfather wanted a quiet, civilized, bourgeois life like he had seen on television. Our newly constructed family did what the folks in AA call "doing a geographic," moving north four hundred miles to Castro Valley to pretend that we had always been an ordinary, intact, nuclear family. ■ The rituals of middle class respectability in that era were easy to mimic. First, the father had to make enough money to have a stay at home wife. Second, the wife had to put herself together every evening and greet the father with a kiss when he came home from a hard day at work. Third, the father was afforded a decompression period in which he could mix himself a martini and drink it in stately silence, without having to deal with the kids or hear too much commotion from the kitchen. And fourth, the entire family would convene in the dining room to eat. Central to the success of this ritual was the satisfactory making of the martini, which had to be ice cold and drunk from one of those "mad men," silver-rimmed, roly poly glasses designed by Dorothy Thorpe. A poorly executed martini could spoil the entire evening. ■ Much to my surprise, children in nice, middle class, white families did not drink. It was many years later when I had my first dry martini.

MARTINI

INGREDIENTS
2 ½ OZ GIN
½ OZ DRY VERMOUTH
1 TO 3 OLIVES FOR GARNISH

PREPARATION
POUR THE INGREDIENTS INTO A MIXING GLASS FILLED WITH ICE CUBES. STIR FOR 30 SECONDS. STRAIN INTO A CHILLED COCKTAIL GLASS. GARNISH WITH OLIVE/S.

In 1967, pretty much worn out from trying to appear normal, I married my high school sweetheart. My family insisted on a large Catholic wedding, even though I was the only one in the family who was even nominally Catholic. My husband and I swore to a Belgian priest, who we could hardly understand, that we would raise all our children Catholic, even though we knew that we were not going to have any. After a large and very long reception, in which a hundred non-italian men pretended to honor the old Sicilian custom of stuffing money down the bride's dress, my newly minted husband and I drove off into the sunset in the direction of the Fairmont Hotel in San Francisco where we had engaged the wedding suite. ■ For some reason, the minute we got settled in our room, going downstairs to the Tonga Room seemed like the most reasonable thing to do. The Tonga Room was one of the greatest of the great tiki bars. Built around the hotel pool, known as the lagoon, it had a floating stage with a Polynesian orchestra, and served drinks

THE TONGA ROOM WAS ONE OF THE GREATEST OF
THE GREAT TIKI BARS. BUILT AROUND THE HOTEL
POOL, KNOWN AS THE LAGOON, IT HAD A FLOATING
STAGE WITH A POLYNESIAN ORCHESTRA

with names like "Zombie," "Singapore Sling,"
"Hurricane," and "Daquiri." The signature drink
was the classic "Mai Tai," which had been served
there with little Chinese umbrellas since 1945.
With over 35 rums, from places like Panama,
Guyana, Jamaica, Trinidad, and St. Croix to
choose from, it was a twenty-year old's idea of
exotic sophistication, and apparently way more
interesting than sex. (It is noteworthy that back-
in-the-day, two well-dressed young people could
get a drink at any upscale bar in San Francisco
without any fear of being carded.) ■ Between the
libations at my wedding reception, and the Mai
Tais at the Tonga Room, I had the only hangover
of my life. To this day, I still feel a little anxious for
my stomach when I see an umbrella in my drink.

MAI TAI

INGREDIENTS
1 OZ LIGHT RUM
1 OZ DARK RUM
½ OZ LIME JUICE
½ OZ ORANGE CURACAO
½ OZ ORGEAT SYRUP
MARASCHINO CHERRY FOR GARNISH

PREPARATION
POUR ALL THE INGREDIENTS EXCEPT
THE DARK RUM INTO A SHAKER
WITH ICE CUBES. SHAKE WELL.
STRAIN INTO AN OLD-FASHIONED
GLASS HALF FILLED WITH ICE.
TOP WITH THE DARK RUM.

OUZO

I COULD SEE THE PARTHENON FROM THE
BEDROOM WINDOW, SO ON THE SECOND DAY,
UNABLE TO TALK MY MATE OUT OF THE LOO,
I VENTURED OUT ALONE TO SEE THE SIGHTS
OF ATHENS AND PONDER MY LIFE CHOICES.

In 1969 I cashed in my student loan check and convinced my husband to take a trip to Greece. We dressed to the nines for our Pan Am flight and spent a good deal of our time lounging at the top deck bar of our stylish new Boeing 747. Flying was different then.

■ On arrival in Athens, we picked up a rental car and headed for the center of town — sort of. No one had told us that all the road signs would be in the Greek alphabet, or that our hotel was on a street whose name started with a triangle. By the time we arrived at our hotel my husband was completely hysterical, and when he also discovered that no one at the hotel spoke English, he locked himself in the bathroom of our suite and did not come out for two days.

I could see the Parthenon from the bedroom window, so on the second day, unable to talk my mate out of the loo, I ventured out alone to see the sights of Athens and ponder my life choices. It was very hot that July 20th, the day that Neil Armstrong stepped out onto the lunar landscape, so I stopped in at a taverna in the Plaka for a cold drink. No one was there but an "elderly" man of around 35 who beckoned me over to his table in a far dark corner. Without talking, he ordered me an Ouzo and showed me how to mix it with water. We sat quietly and companionably for an hour and I left feeling weirdly better. Years later, as he became a counter culture hero, I recognized my drinking companion as Leonard Cohen. It's not surprising that from that day forward he has written the soundtrack to my life.

OUZO

OUZO CAN BE DRUNK STRAIGHT FROM A SHOT GLASS, BUT IS TRADITIONALLY MIXED WITH WATER, AND SERVED OVER ICE IN A SMALL GLASS, WHERE IT TURNS A CLOUDY, BLUE-TINGED WHITE. IT IS ONE OF MANY LICORICE-FLAVORED DIGESTIFS.

The following year, my husband asked if he could choose our vacation destination, and that seemed only fair, until he told me that his idea of a vacation was to hire a snow cat to take us, and a few carelessly chosen friends, behind the snow line to a not-yet-opened resort high in the Sierras called Mono Hot Springs. ■ This collection of rustic cabins and outdoor mineral springs is barely habitable in the summer when it is open and warm, but in the winter, before the roads are passable, it is a little like something out of *The Shining*. Our snow cat picked us up right on schedule, and we loaded six people and their fishing gear into a vehicle made to accommodate four. I got to sit in the seat directly over the exhaust pipe and would have been unbearably nauseated, if I had not been frozen to the bone.

I LOVE JIM BEAM. I LOVE IT NEAT; I LOVE IT IN AN OLD FASHIONED;
I'LL EVEN DRINK IT IN AN AGENT ORANGE OR A JIM'S NUTS,
SO NO ONE HAD TO ASK ME TWICE IF I WOULD LIKE A SWIG.

■ That is when the fellows thought that it would be a good idea to start passing around a fifth of Jim Beam. I love Jim Beam. I love it neat; I love it in an old fashioned; I'll even drink it in an Agent Orange or a Jim's Nuts, so no one had to ask me twice if I would like a swig. Or two. Or three. At 8,000 feet, barreling around in a snow cat in twenty feet of snow, nothing warms the heart more than a shot of whiskey straight out of the bottle with friends. And very few things are dumber.

JIM BEAM

WARNING FROM DIRECTOR OF CLINICAL PHARMACOLOGY AT THE UNIVERSITY OF IOWA, DR. WILLIAM HAYNES: "ALCOHOL IS A VASODILATOR, MEANING THAT IT CAUSES YOUR BLOOD VESSELS TO DILATE, PARTICULARLY THE CAPILLARIES UNDER THE SURFACE OF YOUR SKIN. THUS, THE VOLUME OF BLOOD BROUGHT TO THE SKIN'S SURFACE INCREASES, MAKING YOU FEEL WARM… THIS OVERRIDES ONE OF YOUR BODY'S DEFENSES AGAINST COLD TEMPERATURES, CONSTRICTING YOUR BLOOD VESSELS, THEREBY MINIMIZING BLOOD FLOW TO YOUR SKIN IN ORDER TO KEEP YOUR CORE BODY TEMPERATURE UP." IN PLAIN ENGLISH, DRINKING ALCOHOL WHEN YOU ARE FREEZING IS A GOOD WAY TO DIE OF HYPOTHERMIA. THANKS FELLAS.

26

B
E
E
R

PERHAPS YOU DID NOT KNOW THAT BEERS HAVE A SEXUAL ORIENTATION. THEY DO. AND YOU HAVE TO KEEP UP ON THINGS TO KNOW WHICH BEERS ARE GAY FRIENDLY AND WHICH ARE NOT.

I don't think my experiences in the Sierras had anything to do with my becoming a lesbian, but they might have. I think it had more to do with my having graduated from college in 1972, gotten a divorce, and become Cal. State Hayward's first Women Studies instructor. Teachers become accustomed to the romantic infatuations of their students, but I started to notice that the young people attaching themselves to me were increasingly women, and that my Women Studies colleagues suddenly wanted to meet for drinks in exclusively women's bars. ■ A sad feature of women's bars, in case you have never been in one, is that it is impossible to get a decent cocktail. I suppose this is true of honkytonks and corner bars all over the nation. Order a rusty nail and you will discover that no one knows what you are talking about, or they will inform you that they do not have Drambuie behind the bar, or worst of all, they will make you one with Cutty Sark. It is easier to just order a beer. And if you are in a gay bar, it has to be a gay beer. Perhaps you did not know that beers have a sexual orientation. They do. And you have to keep up on things to know which beers are gay friendly and which are not. San Francisco's Anchor Steam is the gayest beer of all and is always a safe bet. Budweiser is universally boycotted. When in doubt, order a foreign beer. Stella Artois has not come out yet, but everyone knows she is gay.

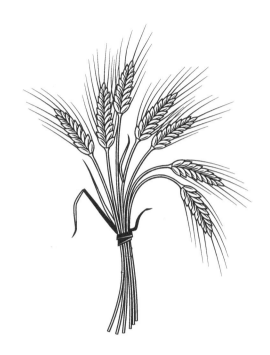

BEER

For collectors of interesting beer bottles, it is not difficult to find gay-themed labels. My most recent favorite was the beer launched by the Scottish craft brewery named Brew Dog for the 2014 Winter Olympics in Sochi. Its name is "Hello, My Name is Vladimir," and the label features images of the Russian president wearing make-up and the slogan, "Not for gays."

Speaking of beer, in 1978, I decided to visit my friends stationed in Germany. The Vietnam War had ended with the Fall of Saigon in 1975, but many of the young men I knew were still in uniform and sending me letters full of the wonders of German Hofbrauhauses. While I imagined going to the Rathaus in Munich, or leaving my heart in Heidelberg, the service men of Frankfort convinced me that all the action was in a little town called Ruedesheim on the Rhine. ■ Ruedesheim is justly famous for its delicious dry white wines, and the Drosselgasses, a crowded little tourist trap of a lane with wall to wall wine bars, but we headed straight for a Hofbrauhaus where it is Oktober all year round, and their motto is not just "It's always

IT TURNS OUT THAT BEER TASTES REALLY GOOD IF YOU THROW
A SHOT OF GREEN WALDMEISTER OR RASPBERRY SYRUP INTO
IT, AND BECAUSE IT GOES DOWN SO EASILY, YOU CAN HARDLY
TELL HOW MUCH EFFECT IT IS HAVING ON YOUR JUDGMENT.

five o'clock somewhere," but "It's always five o'clock here." The spectacularly talented and well-endowed serving wenches, who could carry ten giant beer steins with ease, were undoubtedly the inspiration for the hiring practices and philosophy of Hooters circa 1983 in the United States: "delightfully tacky, yet unrefined." ■ It turns out that beer tastes really good if you throw a shot of green waldmeister or raspberry syrup into it, and because it goes down so easily, you can hardly tell how much effect it is having on your judgment. I never even noticed when the feminist part of me that was outraged by the objectification of the buxom barmaids, gave way to the lesbian part of me that was praying, with lieutenant Chuck and his buddies, for a wardrobe malfunction.

BERLINER WEISSE MIT SCHUSS

INGREDIENTS
1 OZ RED-RASPBERRY FLAVORED SYRUP (OR GREEN
WALDMEISTER SWEET WOODRUFF SYRUP)
16 OZS LIGHT GERMAN WHEAT BEER

PREPARATION
POUR A 1 OZ SCHUSS OF WALDMEISTER OR RASPBER-
RY SYRUP INTO A LARGE WHEAT-BEER GLASS. SLOWLY
ADD 16 OZS COLD BERLINER WEISSE OR OTHER LIGHT
GERMAN-STYLE WHEAT BEER.

…MY PLAN WAS TO TAKE A HALF BOTTLE OF CALIFORNIA CABERNET DOWN TO THE TIDE POOLS TO CATCH THE SUNSET IN SOLITARY SPLENDOR, AND THEN TO SCURRY UP TO THE LODGE TO JOIN THE OTHERS AND HEAR THE MOST SALIENT PARTS OF MR. CAMPBELL'S SPEECH.

In 1981, I went to a conference of the National Council of Teachers of English specifically to hear the keynote speaker, the renowned American mythologist Joseph Campbell. He was the most beloved public intellectual in the nation, author of *The Hero with a Thousand Faces*, and more importantly the man who told an entire generation to just "Follow [their] bliss." Although we didn't quite understand what he was saying, we tried our best to follow his exhortation. ■ The event was held at the beautiful Asilomar conference grounds, just south of the Monterey peninsula, on a magnificent stretch of dunes resplendent with non-native ice plant, which has long since been replaced by less inspiring indigenous grasses. On the night of Campbell's address, the sand and the surf were made even more irresistible by a red/orange sunset the likes of which can only be seen in California when the pollution is just right. ■ I was sorely torn between sunset and satori, so I decided that I might be able to satisfy both my senses and my intellect: My plan was to take a half bottle of California cabernet down to the tide pools to catch the sunset in solitary splendor, and then to scurry up to the lodge to join the others and hear the most salient parts of Mr. Campbell's speech. ■ It was all working perfectly. I had the beach completely to myself; the sunset was reaching perfection; and the cabernet and I were getting in the zone, when I was annoyed to hear a man behind me say, "Beautiful, isn't it." I really wanted to ignore him, but he had the most kindly and sort of tuned-in voice, so I replied, "Very. I should really be up at the lodge listening to an important speaker, but I couldn't resist coming down here first." He smiled slightly and said, "Me too, but don't worry, as long as you get there before I do, you won't be late."

CABERNET

CALIFORNIA CABERNETS ARE A MOVING TARGET, BUT YOU CAN ALWAYS FIND AN EXCELLENT RECOMMENDATION FOR THAT SPECIAL DINNER PARTY OR IMPROMPTU TRIP TO THE BEACH AT THE CALIFORNIA CABERNET SOCIETY, "AN ALLIANCE OF WINERIES COMMITTED TO EXPANDING WORLDWIDE REGARD AND APPRECIATION FOR CALIFORNIA CABERNET SAUVIGNON." WWW. CALIFORNIACABERNETSOCIETY.COM.

… I HAVE TASTED PORT IN THE CAVES OF OPORTO, PORTUGAL; BUT I HAVE NEVER BEEN SO WARMED BY A GLASS OF PORT AS THE ONE SENT TO ME BY THE HUNT MASTER OF HALSTED.

In the Winter semester of 1982 I took a sabbatical, and for some reason thought it would be a good idea to take a road trip around Britain. There were two things wrong with this plan. First, England is really cold in December; and second, it turned out my travelling companion had a drinking problem, so in order to see anything, and not spend all our time in pubs, we had to carry a boot full of beer in the car. Yes, after a month in England, one starts to call the trunk of the car a boot. ■ The English countryside is beautiful, even in the cold, and even when you have to see it from the wrong side of the road. We had the castles and manor houses to ourselves, especially as we wound our way up to the frigid north — think Game of Thrones. I wanted to drive Hadrian's Wall from Chester to Newcastle and it was somewhere midway that I caught drift of a real English hunt. ■ We got up at an ungodly hour and parked the car close enough to take pictures, but far enough away not to engage with the surly bunch of commoners who seemed to be bearing a deep ancestral grudge against the gathering lords and ladies. I watched in wonder as the horses, dogs and hunters, in beautiful red livery, arranged themselves. Then I could see their leader riding towards me; but instead of asking me politely, as I expected, to leave, the gentleman bent down and asked me if it was my first hunt. When I said yes, he informed me that it was customary for first timers to give the Hunt Master a kiss for good luck. What could a girl do? Shortly after, a lady arrived with a tray of hot canapés and vintage port. ■ I have had a glass of port sitting in the prize window of the Carnelian room in San Francisco, looking down on the Pyramid building; I have tasted port in the Caves of Oporto, Portugal; but I have never been so warmed by a glass of port as the one sent to me by the Hunt Master of Halsted.

PORT

YOUNG VINTAGE PORTS (LESS THAN 5 YEARS OLD) CAN OFTEN LAST 4-5 DAYS ONCE OPENED. HOWEVER, OLDER VINTAGE PORTS (MORE THAN 15 YEARS OLD) ARE NOT MEANT TO BE LEFT OPEN FOR MORE THAN 2-3 DAYS. REALLY OLD VINTAGE PORTS (MORE THAN 25 YEARS OLD) ARE AT THEIR BEST IF CONSUMED WITHIN 24-48 HOURS. I CAN ATTEST TO THE FACT THAT ALL OF THE PORT OPENED ON THE MORNING OF THE HUNT WAS CONSUMED BY NOON.

Meanwhile, my lovely ex-husband and I continued to be friends, and he developed a real adventurous streak and a love of travel. Go figure. We would often grab our current partners and spend a week in sunny Puerto Vallarta seeing the sights, fishing, and of course drinking the local tequila. We loved Blancos in shots or in authentic Margaritas made with just fresh lime juice and Controy, Mexico's answer to Cointreau. ■ One year while searching the docks for a fishing boat to go out and chase down some Mahi Mahi, we met a fellow with a decent looking yacht, who told us he could take us to a private beach, just south of Yelapa, reachable only by small boat. He promised to serve us lunch and introduce us to real native Mezcal made right in the jungles above his little cove. We engaged his services for the next day, and came equipped with beach towels and great attitudes. ■ True to his word, he served us a simple but delicious lunch of grilled fish

THE MEZCAL WAS A LITTLE LIKE TRUTH SERUM, BRINGING OUT
THE HALLUCINATORY ESSENCE OF EACH OF US. FOR MY PART, I
SPENT THE REST OF THE AFTERNOON IN DEEP CONVERSATION
WITH THE MANGIEST DOG I HAVE EVEN SEEN,

and rice. Then he disappeared into the jungle for a couple hours, only to return holding a very strange looking, mouth blown bottle. He set it on the table, poured himself a healthy glassful, and said he would be napping until we woke him up to go home. ■ The Mezcal was a little like truth serum, bringing out the hallucinatory essence of each of us. For my part, I spent the rest of the afternoon in deep conversation with the mangiest dog I have even seen, who in the photo someone snapped of us, appears to be listening to me in rapt attention.

FRESH START

IF YOU DO NOT HAVE THE ATMOSPHERICS OF A TROPICAL BEACH AND AN ADORING CANINE, YOU MIGHT LIKE TO TRY YOUR MESCAL IN A COCKTAIL. MY FAVORITE IS THIS ONE CUT OUT OF AN OLD ISSUE OF GQ MAGAZINE AND REVISED WITH MY FAVORITE LIQUORS. I CALL IT FRESH START.

INGREDIENTS
2 OZ ST. ALBANS MEZCAL
¾ OZ LUSTAU EAST INDIA SALERA SHERRY
¼ OZ ALLPICE DRAM
1 DASH ANGOSTURA BITTERS
1 DASH REGAN'S ORANGE BITTERS # 6

PREPARATION
STIR INGREDIENTS TOGETHER IN AN ICE-FILLED OLD-FASHIONED GLASS. GARNISH WITH A LEMON TWIST.

WALKING DOWN A DARK STREET IN LISBON ONE NIGHT, I SAW A SMALL, GREEN BOTTLE, SHAPED LIKE A BULLET, IN A LIQUOR STORE WINDOW. IT WAS A DOUBLE SHOT OF ABSINTHE WAITING TO BE TASTED.

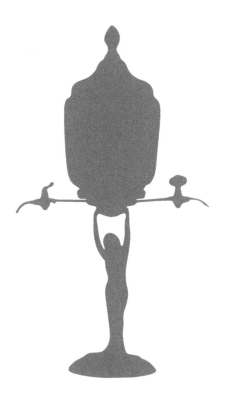

When it comes to hallucinogenic liquors though, nothing can compete with Absinthe, or my ignorance about it. I was a literature major, and all I knew about "the green fairy," had been gleaned from the fanciful accounts of the likes of Rimbuad, Verlaine, Oscar Wilde and Ernest Hemingway. Because it had been banned in the United States in 1915, I had never even seen a bottle of it. ■ But then in 1986, I took a trip to Portugal, where I discovered Fado dancing, giant langostino, and Absinthe. Though Europe also participated in the banning of the licorice-flavored liquor, Spain and Portugal had just ignored the whole question. I have read since that the hallucinatory effects of the wormwood in Absinthe were vastly exaggerated, but you can't prove that by me. ■ Walking down a dark street in Lisbon one night, I saw a small, green bottle, shaped like a bullet, in a liquor store window. It was a double shot of Absinthe waiting to be tasted. I did not know the ritual of the slotted spoon and the cube of sugar, which is now more often associated with French Pastis, so I went back to my hotel room and downed the whole thing. When I woke up thirty hours later, I had a roaring headache and the sense that I could write deep, dark poetry like Baudelaire.

ABSINTHE

PRODUCTION OF ABSINTHE STARTED UP AGAIN IN THE 1990'S WHEN MOST COUNTRIES DROPPED THEIR BANS ON ITS SALE AND CONSUMPTION. WHEN DRUNK CORRECTLY AND IN MODERATION, IT IS QUITE A PLEASANT APERITIF. NOWADAYS, EVEN THE READER/WRITERS OF WIKIPEDIA KNOW HOW TO DRINK ABSINTHE CORRECTLY: "TRADITIONALLY, ABSINTHE IS PREPARED BY PLACING A SUGAR CUBE ON TOP OF A SPECIALLY DESIGNED SLOTTED SPOON, AND THEN PLACING THE SPOON ON THE GLASS WHICH HAS BEEN FILLED WITH A MEASURE OF ABSINTHE. ICED WATER IS THEN POURED OR DRIPPED OVER THE SUGAR CUBE IN A MANNER WHEREBY THE WATER IS SLOWLY AND EVENLY DISPLACED INTO THE ABSINTHE, SUCH THAT THE FINAL PREPARATION CONTAINS 1 PART ABSINTHE AND 3-5 PARTS WATER.

I HAD WHAT HENRY JAMES CALLED "AN AESTHETIC HEADACHE." AND WHEN I SAW A SIGN THAT SAID *STANZA PER AFFITTO*, WHICH I WAS PRAYING MEANT ROOM FOR RENT, I PULLED DIRECTLY INTO THE CARPORT AND THREW A SMALL, SATISFYING, MOSTLY PRIVATE TANTRUM.

The following summer I decided to connect with my roots and visit Sicily. It was impossible to track down my relatives, since I did not even know my father's real name, but I soon discovered that the term mafia is not used in Sicily. No, my father was apparently a member of the "Cosa Nostra" (Our Thing), or "The Honoured Society" or the "Men of Respect." ■ I rented a cranky, aging Fiat in Palermo from "a made man," and began to circumnavigate the island, where all the women looked, I must admit, an awful lot like me. From Syracuse to Agrigento to Catania, I braved the coastal highways and the bi-polar Sicilian drivers, marveling at the Greek temples and the Byzantine art, until suddenly, without warning, I could not drive another mile. I went all "Sicilian" myself with fatigue and frustration. I had what Henry

GRAPPA

GRAPPA IS MADE FROM THE BYPROD-
UCTS OF WINE PRODUCTION AND
VARIES WILDLY FROM SOMETHING
APPROACHING RUBBING ALCOHOL
TO AMBROSIA. IT IS ONE LIQUOR
WHERE IT PAYS TO BUY THE BEST
BOTTLE YOU CAN AFFORD. A GREAT
WAY TO DISCOVER A GRAPPA THAT
SUITS YOUR TASTE IS TO ORDER A
FLIGHT OF GRAPPAS AT A GOOD
RESTAURANT LIKE JARDINIERE IN
SAN FRANCISCO. MAKE YOUR OWN
TASTING NOTES AND BUY A BOTTLE
OF THE ONE YOU LIKE BEST. I LOVE
A GRAPPA MADE FROM MOSCATO
GRAPES.

James called "an aesthetic headache." And when I saw a sign that said *stanza per affitto*, which I was praying meant room for rent, I pulled directly into the carport and threw a small, satisfying, mostly private tantrum. ■ I rented that stanza, above the carport, above Isola Bella, the most beautiful bay in the world, for a week, never moving the Fix-It-Again-Tony even once. Consequently, for seven consecutive nights, I ate at the nearest trattoria, where each night they delighted me with fresh sardines, spaghetti arrabiata, artichoke hearts in butter, and exquisite local wines. On my last night there, as a farewell gift, they poured fulsome shots of Grappa for me to try, and since I had never had any problem with anything anyone had ever given me to drink, I followed my host's lead, clinked glasses, and shouted Salute! It was then and there that I realized there was a God, and she was Sicilian.

IF YOU SHOULD COME ACROSS SOME HUNDRED-YEAR-OLD
BRANDY, PLEASE DRINK IT WARMED IN THE LARGEST SNIFTER
YOU CAN FIND. BUT IF YOU ENJOY YOUR BRANDY IN A COCKTAIL,
I RECOMMEND THIS VERSION OF THE *VIEUX CARRE*.

This is a story of thwarted love and one hundred year old brandy. When I was in college I fell madly in love with my charismatic and universally respected Biblical Literature professor. I worked hard to distinguish myself in his eyes, and wrote papers that I thought were deep and original. Most probably the deep papers were not very original, and the original papers were not very deep, but I treasured his crabbed comments, and the giant red A's he fashioned with his bold-nibbed fountain pen. He was a scholar, a wrestler, and a connoisseur of Spanish art; he grew orchids and drove a motorcycle; even as a delusional adolescent, I could not imagine a scenario in which he would choose to spend time with me. ■ Fifteen years later, a published professor myself, I re-visited my alma mater and was curious to see the object of my youthful infatuation. He was older, but still charming, and much to my surprise, remembered my name. He had a copy of Bosch's triptych *The Garden of Earthly Delights* on an easel in his office, and we started to discuss it, just as if we were equals. Within minutes, he told me that his wife had left him and that he would like to have dinner with me. It was then that I remembered that I was a lesbian. To which he said, "Well, that is your business, isn't it." So sophisticated. Then he pointed out that he was 30 years older than me, and I tried on a bit of sophistication myself, "Well, that is your business, isn't it." ■ For three months I nurtured the pleasant fantasy that he admired me for my quick and subtle mind, and not just for my youthful body. Unfortunately, one day I made the mistake of asking him about a salient point I had made in one of my graduate papers, and it was clear that he did not remember a single thing that I had ever written. Or said. That rankled. ■ Shortly after, he asked me to marry him, and follow him into retirement to his casa on the southern coast of Spain. For weeks, my friends kept up a continuous chorus of "Get the Villa." It was tempting. But luckily, I knew that I was too young, and too gay, and not really a match for him--yet. We parted amicably over a hundred year old bottle of Brandy de Jerez, which had been given to him by the King of Spain for work he had done authenticating important works by Spanish painters. A few months later, he married the English Department secretary. Every few years I get a lovely gift in the mail from him. Once he sent me a coin that had been used by Queen Isabella to fund Christopher Columbus's voyage to the Americas.

VIEUX CARRE

INGREDIENTS:
3/4 OZ RYE WHISKEY
3/4 OZ BRANDY/COGNAC
3/4 OZ SWEET VERMOUTH
DASH PEYCHAUD'S BITTERS
DASH ANGOSTURA BITTERS
1/2 TSP BENEDICTINE
CHERRY FOR GARNISH

PREPARATION
COMBINE THE INGREDIENTS IN A MIXING GLASS FILLED WITH ICE. STIR WELL. STRAIN INTO AN OLD-FASHIONED GLASS FILLED WITH ICE. GARNISH WITH A CHERRY.

In the summer of 1995, I made a visit to Turkey to see the western reforms of Kemal Ataturk in action, to visit the site of the Trojan war, to enjoy the spectacularly intact Greek ruins, to visit the church of Saint Nicholas, and to snorkel in the pristine waters of the Turquoise Coast, amidst the sunken artifacts of ancient cities. As far as the Turks were concerned, I had come primarily to look at hundreds of hand-knotted rugs, and to drink prodigious amounts of the ubiquitous Turkish tea. ■ When in Istanbul, I stayed at a small boutique hotel called The Empress Zoe. My Spartan, but oddly chic, room was reached by a two story spiral staircase that went on for another two flights to an outdoor, rooftop, dining room where the uniquely robust Turkish breakfast was served each morning: magnificent black and green olives, feta and kashkavai cheeses, cucumbers, sweet peppers, hard boiled eggs, fresh baked white bread, honey, fruit preserves and the first cup of strong, black tea of the day.

WHILE I WAS WAITING FOR THE LAST LIGHT OF DAY TO DISAPPEAR, AND FOR THE VOICES TO INTONE, SOMEONE, EVEN QUIETER THAN MYSELF, PLACED A BOTTLE OF RAKI AND SOME MEZE ON MY TABLE AND POLITELY WITHDREW.

■ The hotel was beautifully situated between the Blue Mosque and Santa Sophia; each and every *ezan*, or call to prayer, was a stereophonic wonder. So one balmy night I decided to sneak up the circular stairs to the hotel rooftop to enjoy the 6th *ezan*, called *Yatsi*, in perfect, prayerful solitude. While I was waiting for the last light of day to disappear, and for the voices to intone, someone, even quieter than myself, placed a bottle of Raki and some meze on my table and politely withdrew. ■ At 10:08 pm the call to prayer commenced. The lights shone on the minarets. The Raki was sweet with anise and strong. I did not notice how strong (100 proof) until I tried to negotiate the spiral stairs back to my room. I am afraid I disturbed two other guests before I found the right lock to put my key in.

RAKI

RAKI IS DRUNK STRAIGHT, OR WITH WATER, VERY MUCH LIKE OUZO OR ABSINTHE. DILUTION WITH WATER CAUSES RAKI TO TURN A MILKY-WHITE. IN TURKEY, THE DRINK IS POPULARLY REFERRED TO AS ASLAN SÜTÜ (LION'S MILK). METAPHORICALLY, A TURKISH LION IS A COURAGEOUS MAN, SO THIS IS APPROPRIATELY MILK FOR AN ALPHA MALE.

SINGAPORE SLING

I HEADED STRAIGHT FOR THE LONG BAR AT RAFFLES AND ORDERED A SINGAPORE SLING, WHICH LOOKED SOMEWHAT DEPRESSINGLY LIKE A SHIRLEY TEMPLE, AND REMINDED ME OF HOW LITTLE PROGRESS WE REALLY MAKE IN THIS WORLD, NO MATTER HOW MUCH WE FLAP OUR ARMS AROUND.

In 1996, in a last ditch effort to save our fourteen year relationship, my partner and I decided to get away from it all and take a romantic cruise in Indonesia. This was a bad idea for a number of reasons. First, my partner did not particularly like travelling, even under the best of conditions. Second, Indonesia is one giant tourist trap surrounded by unbelievable squalor. And third, there is nothing like being cramped into an 8x10 room for three weeks with someone you are not very fond of at the moment. At least we avoided the cliché of having a break-up baby. ■ Despite all the reasons to be grumpy, I made things extra stressful by insisting on going ahead and having a good time. In Bali, I wrapped myself in the traditional red-checkered skirts, which reminded me of Sicilian tablecloths, and joined in the native dances. In Java, I climbed the temple at Borobodur and had a semi-religious experience (perhaps heatstroke?). In Sumatra, I sat on an orangutan's lap, and watched a fourteen foot komodo dragon lick his lips just a chicken wire fence away. In Kuala Lumpur I handled poisonous pit vipers in a Hindu temple. In Singapore I finally realized that no amount of entertaining myself to death was going to fix the relationship, so I headed straight for the Long Bar at Raffles and ordered a Singapore Sling, which

SINGAPORE SLING

INGREDIENTS
1/2 OZ GRENADINE SYRUP
1 OZ GIN
SWEET AND SOUR MIX
CLUB SODA
1/2 OZ CHERRY BRANDY

PREPARATION
POUR GRENADINE INTO THE BOTTOM OF A COLLINS GLASS, AND FILL WITH ICE. ADD GIN. ALMOST-FILL WITH EQUAL PARTS OF SWEET AND SOUR AND CHILLED SODA. TOP WITH CHERRY BRANDY. SERVE UNSTIRRED. GARNISHED WITH A CHERRY.

looked somewhat depressingly like a Shirley Temple, and reminded me of how little progress we really make in this world, no matter how much we flap our arms around.

In the summer of 1997, I was selected by the International Education Committee of my college to take a group of students to Costa Rica to see the sights and learn a little something about the world. Officially, I was there to teach a course on travel photography; unofficially, my main duty was to bring them all back alive. ■ This is not as easy as it sounds. Imagine herding sixteen teenagers in a foreign country which is famous for its biodiversity. Biodiversity is a euphemism for 139 species of snakes, of which 22 are venomous. Biodiversity is code for tarantulas, scorpions, crocodiles, caiman, and seriously poisonous frogs. Biodiversity is just branding for a Bullet Ant whose bite feels like — well you know. Even the abundant fauna in Costa Rica wants you dead. ■ And the epicenter of biodiversity in Costa Rica is Tortuguero National Park, where we had booked a jungle resort with tent cabins spaced irregularly across acres of viper and red ant infested jungle. At dinner the first night, I was puzzled about how I was going to keep my students from sneaking out for a midnight swim, or just visiting each other's tents, and falling victim to some

BIODIVERSITY IS CODE FOR TARANTULAS, SCORPIONS, CROCODILES, CAIMAN, AND SERIOUSLY POISONOUS FROGS.

form of biodiversity I hadn't even heard of yet. So I gave the green light to an after dinner glass of Guaro, hoping that the national liquor of Costa Rica would be strong enough to make them drowsy and disinclined to wander. That's when Andrew, asserting his budding masculinity, challenged me to a drinking game. If he won, the students could take their flashlights out and go to the beach to look at the turtle eggs (one of them would undoubtedly die, and I would never teach again); if I won, they had to stay in their tents all night and wait for the expert guide to take us out on the scheduled turtle viewing the following night (making them cranky, but probably saving their lives). ■ I will always remember my relief later that night, lying in the cozy hammock of my tent, twenty feet off the ground, howler monkeys jabbering away, but above it all the sound of Andrew throwing up into the moist jungle night air, and knowing that all my students were safe in their beds.

GUARO SOUR

IF YOU ARE NOT ENGAGED IN A LIFE OR DEATH DRINKING MATCH, WHICH OF COURSE REQUIRES STRAIGHT SHOTS, YOU MIGHT ENJOY THIS TRADITIONAL GUARO SOUR COCKTAIL.

INGREDIENTS
2 OZ GUARO (CACIQUE GUARO. THE ONLY LEGAL BRAND IN COSTA RICA)
2 OZS SIMPLE SYRUP OR 2 TEASPOONS RAW SUGAR
1 LIME CUT INTO 6 OR 8 WEDGES
ICE CUBES, AS NEEDED | SPLASH OF CLUB SODA

PREPARATION
PUT GUARO, SUGAR AND LIME WEDGES IN A ROCKS GLASS. MUDDLE ALL THE INGREDIENTS UNTIL THE JUICE IS EXTRACTED AND THE RINDS ARE BRUISED. LEAVE IT ALL IN THE GLASS AND ADD ICE CUBES. TOP WITH A SPLASH OF CLUB SODA. SERVE WITH A STRAW.

J
A
M
E
S
O
N

I
R
I
S
H

W
H
I
S
K
E
Y

I BECAME A REGULAR AT THE DISTILLERY, TAKING THE
TOUR IN ONCE A DAY AT 4PM, IN HOPES OF BEING CHOSEN
TO TAKE PART IN THEIR TUTORED WHISKEY TASTING.

In 2004, I got caught up in the outsourcing craze, and ended up for a month in Dublin, Ireland. Now Dublin is a very fine town, and I enjoyed visiting Dublin Castle, perusing the Book of Kells at Trinity College, and cruising the pubs around St. Stephens' Green, but nothing was as fun as the guided tours at the Guinness Brewery, where they finish off every complimentary glass of beer with a foam shamrock, or the Jameson Distillery, where you can earn an Irish Whiskey Taster's Certificate. ■ I became a regular at the distillery, taking the tour in once a day at 4pm, in hopes of being chosen to take part in their tutored whiskey tasting. When my turn finally came, I was set down with three whiskeys, one American, one Scottish, and one Irish. The trick of course was to prefer the Jameson to all comers. That was not too difficult as the first glass was clearly Jim Beam, which

though I love it on a snow cat in the Sierras, was kind of a cheap shot on their part (pun intended). The second dram was a scotch whiskey of the "I just licked a charred log right out of the fire" variety. An acquired taste for most people, to be sure, but one of my favorites. And the last glass was an absolutely perfect 18 year old Jameson blend. I named the Jim Beam, guessed at the Laphroig, and correctly preferred the aged Jameson. I still keep my Whiskey Taster Certificate proudly in my fire safe with all my important papers, right next to my gun registration, my master's degree diploma, and my divorce papers.

JAMESON IRISH WHISKEY

To be a real master blender or whiskey taster, you have to be able to discern, and more importantly, name a bewildering array of tastes and smells. Here is the way Jameson characterizes its own 18 year old blend:

Nose: Aromatic oils with a touch of wood, spicy toffee.

Taste: Wonderfully mellow and smooth, a mouthful of complex flavour — fudge, toffee, spice, hints of wood and leather, vanilla and a gentle sherry nuttiness.

Finish: A long, lingering finish carries the theme of the wood, spice and toffee right through to the end.

STREGA PINK WITCH

MANY OF MY CATS HAVE HAD TO SUFFER SUCH INDIGNITIES. ONE CAN DRESS A DOG UP ALL DAY LONG, BUT PUT A FUNNY HAT ON A CAT JUST ONCE AND SHE WILL NEVER FORGIVE YOU.

I got my first cat because I needed to clear the mice out of an old Victorian in San Francisco. This cat was feral, living in a barn, and tried to eviscerate me when I caught her, so I thought she was up to the job, and she was. But once she cleared the house of varmints, she dusted off her fur, pulled in her claws and became a total lap princess. I named her Blanco, because she was pure white, had a rough start, and a smooth finish. She was the first of many cats named for my favorite liquors. ■ My next cat was a calico so I named her Mai Tai. When she was a kitten, I took a picture of her in a big cocktail glass, complete with a paper umbrella. Many of my cats have had to suffer such indignities. One can dress a dog up all day long, but put a funny hat on a cat just once and she will never forgive you. ■ Strega was named after Sicily's premier liquor; she was all black sugar and licorice with yellow eyes. When called to the shelter to save this little black witches' familiar from being euthanized, I saw the photographic possibilities immediately, and even though I remembered that my father shared the gambler's suspicion about black cats and crossed paths, I brought her home and popped her into a carved-out pumpkin and started shooting like crazy. I'm embarrassed to say that even though I'm quite a good photographer, the only images I have been able to sell on a regular basis are holiday cat cards.

STREGA PINK WITCH

INGREDIENTS
2 PARTS GIN
1 PART STREGA
4 PARTS PINK GRAPEFRUIT JUICE

PREPARATION
SHAKE WITH ICE AND STRAIN INTO A TALL GLASS.

BAIJIU IS MADE FROM GLUTINOUS RICE, AND IT MAKES
MOONSHINE SEEM LIKE MOTHER'S BREAST MILK.

My first trip to China with students was in 1999, so in 2005 when my college needed a delegation to check out a sister college relationship with a school in Taizhou, I was onboard for the maiden visit. My college, having read some outdated tourist guide, sent out a memo to the delegates saying that all the female faculty must wear dresses, and the lone male Dean had to wear a suit. I immediately informed them that I would be happy to wear a suit and tie, but would not be wearing a dress. The Dean didn't go so far as to say he would wear a dress, but he did refuse to wear a tie. The consequence of our little sartorial uprising was that when I arrived in Taizhou, resplendent in a handsomely tailored blue blazer, and greeted everyone with a well practiced *nî hâo*, the Chinese assumed that I was the group leader. ■ Western women, even those wearing dresses, tend to look clunky and masculine next to the delicate and feminine women of urban China, so it quickly became clear that the Chinese also thought that I might be a guy. When my female counterparts were given extravagant bouquets, I was presented with a glass "trophy." These differences were particularly noticeable at the many banquets we attended. ■ I was always seated in the chair for the honored quest, facing the door, and next to the host. I was always served first from the banquet plates, and I was always given the fish eye before the rest of the whole fish could be served. Most interestingly, I was always included in the after dinner drinking games, much to the disapproval of the lone female faculty member on the Chinese side, who was clearly excluded, and the consternation of my Dean, who was after all, if not the acting leader, at least a legitimate man.

■ These drinking sessions included games that I had never seen, but looked vaguely familiar, and required a flashing of fingers and hands before somebody lost and had to down a shot of the 120 proof liquor called Baijiu. Baijiu is made from glutinous rice, and it makes moonshine seem like mother's breast milk. Luckily, my host kept score for me, and nudged me soundly when it was my turn to drink. By the end of the festivities, I was really glad that I was the leader, and was beginning to wonder if I might also be a guy?

BAIJIU

BAIJIU IS A WHITE LIQUOR, AND OFTEN LIKENED TO VODKA. IT SOME-TIMES COMES IN CHARMING CERAMIC BOTTLES, WHICH LOOK LIKE FINE KOREAN PORCELAINS. IT IS SAID THAT YOU CAN SUBSTITUTE BAIJIU FOR VODKA IN ANY RECIPE THAT CALLS FOR IT — BUT I WOULDN'T. DRINK IT STRAIGHT LIKE MAN, OR DON'T DRINK IT AT ALL.

W
K
D

O
R
I
G
I
N
A
L

V
O
D
K
A

AS MUCH AS I WAS TOUCHED BY MY STUDENT'S TRIBUTE, I CAN THINK OF ABSOLUTELY NOTHING ELSE GOOD TO SAY ABOUT A DRINK THAT COMES IN COLORS, NOT FLAVORS.

In 2006 fresh off my remarkable success in Taizhou, China, I was chosen to take 18 teenagers to Sydney, Australia for their four month long semester abroad. I relished the idea of going somewhere warm where the Opera House was a bigger draw than the biodiversity. But oddly enough, our first real mishap occurred just a week into the trip when we visited a nature preserve on the way to the famous Jana caves. My lovely hearing impaired student must have misinterpreted the ASL sign for "don't skritch the Koala on the backside," because she was fairly severely mauled on the arm after giving a friendly looking Quantas mascot a pat on the butt. My first aid skills came in handy that day, and I started to get a reputation among the students as someone who knew how to do stuff. ■ This notion took even further hold weeks later when I met them all at a pub at the train station in Sydney for a drink and proceeded to run the pool table for an hour against all comers. And then there was the poker game, where the fellows asked me if I knew how to play, and invited me to join in their game. I said I'd play if they would please write down the order of the winning hands for me, and it wasn't until I had all the chips that they realized they had been seriously had. ■ It was around the last month of the trip that I was surprised to see that the students had adopted a local alcopop called WKD as their signature drink. It sort of made sense, as WKD was heavily advertised to appeal to underage drinkers with the slogan "Have you got a WKD side" (Have you got a wicked side). I was even fairly happy with their choice since WKD contains only 3.5% ABV, and was even less likely to get them in trouble than the excellent local beers. There was something oddly gleeful though about the way that they embraced this brand, which I didn't

understand until long after the trip was over, and a student confessed to me that whenever the students got into a tight spot, they would invoke the WKD slogan, which for them was, "What Would Katona Do."

WKD ORIGINAL VODKA

As much as I was touched by my student's tribute, I can think of absolutely nothing else good to say about a drink that comes in colors, not flavors. So I will refer you to WKD's own advertising literature: "Launched in 1996, WKD comes in six irresistible variants consisting of Original Blue, Iron Brew, Orange, Green, Purple and Red—all very different, very refreshing and made from an alcoholic mix of deliciousness and WKD-ness." And "What Would Katona Do" if she was ever in Australia again? Order one of the outstanding Aussie beers.

THE BEST MUDSLIDE I'VE EVER HAD WAS THE CULMINATION OF A NEAR PERFECT DAY IN PARADISE AT THE HILTON WAIKOLOA VILLAGE HOTEL.

I make a distinction between serious travel and vacation. Serious travel involves a salary or an epiphany. When I'm in New Delhi teaching the locals to sound like Americans so that they can get a job answering the phone for L. L. Bean, that is serious travel. When I take a side trip to Haridwar, and engage my own personal guru to help me float a basket of leaves and marigolds down the Ganges at midnight, that is serious travel. But when I just pack a toothbrush, a snorkel mask and a beach towel, that is a vacation. ■ Vacation towns have their own special drink vocabularies. Margaritas and tequila shooters in Key West; Banana Monkeys in Cancun; Captain Morgan's Rum with various exotic juices in Belize; and Mudslides and Lava Flows on the big island of Hawaii. I do not know why people drink silly drinks, with sillier names, in the tropics, but I do know why they don garishly printed shirts. ■ The best mudslide I've ever had was the culmination of a near perfect day in paradise at the Hilton Waikoloa Village Hotel. My travelling companion had managed to win the dolphin lottery, and we had spent the early part of the day cavorting with an Atlantic Bottlenose Dolphin named Ohana. From there we hit all the pools and water features, and finally put on some fashionably gauzy white clothes to cruise around the hotel's private lagoon. Somewhere along the line we disembarked at a happening little bar and ordered mudslides — plural. They arrived overflowing with heavy cream and rich, dark, chocolate syrup. I have only one suggestion for anyone considering ordering more than one mudslide in an evening — wear a gaily-printed tropical shirt whose background colors are white and brown.

MUDSLIDE

INGREDIENTS:
1 OZ VODKA
1 OZ KAHLUA
1 OZ BAILEYS IRISH CREAM
1 OZ MILK OR CREAM
1 CUP ICE
CHOCOLATE SYRUP (OPTIONAL)

PREPARATION
ADD ALL THE INGREDIENTS (EXCEPT CHOCOLATE SYRUP) INTO A BLENDER. BLEND UNTIL SMOOTH. POUR THE CONTENTS OF THE BLENDER INTO A LARGE HURRICANE GLASS.
(OPTIONAL: LINE THE GLASS WITH CHOCOLATE SYRUP BEFORE ADDING THE OTHER INGREDIENTS OR DRIZZLE CHOCOLATE SYRUP ON TOP)

C
H
A
M
P
A
G
N
E

… I TOASTED WITH A GLASS
OF CHAMPAGNE WHEN I GOT
MARRIED, WHEN I GRADUATED
FROM COLLEGE, WHEN I GOT MY
FIRST TEACHING JOB, AND WHEN
I BOUGHT MY FIRST HOME — I
LOVE THAT CHARACTERISTIC
SOUND OF A POPPING CORK.

If there is one drink that is universally associated with gaiety and celebration, it has to be champagne. I know I toasted with a glass of champagne when I got married, when I graduated from college, when I got my first teaching job, and when I bought my first home — l love that characteristic sound of a popping cork. But my favorite glass of champagne was an imaginary one I had in Shanghai on New Year's Eve in 2009. ■ It was freezing that December in China, and it felt like my best friend and I had all of Shanghai to ourselves, except of course for a couple billion Chinese. Our one conundrum was to find a place where we could enjoy the New Year's Eve fireworks without getting trampled to death on the Bund. This would of course be the western New Year, not to be confused with the Chinese New Year, Gung Hay Fat Choy, celebrated in February.

■ We were lucky to be staying at the Shanghai Marriott near where the fireworks would be set off, but our room did not have a good view of the night sky. So we decided, through a series of exaggerated and largely nonsensical gestures, to beg the mandarin-speaking ladies in the rooftop spa to leave the door open for us that night. Much to our amazement, they had understood us, and even left the slider to the outside balcony unlocked. It was there, thirty-seven stories high, bundled up against the frigid night air and piercing wind, that we saw the extravagant fireworks and light show, and most especially the thousands of candle lanterns floating upwards and away. I ordered an imaginary bottle of Taittinger from room service, and as we watched the clocks all over the city register midnight, we hoisted our invisible champagne flutes to ring in the best New Year ever.

MIMOSA

IF YOU HAVE A REALLY NICE BOTTLE OF CHAMPAGNE, YOU WILL WANT TO PUT IT ON ICE IN YOUR FAVORITE ICE BUCKET AND DRINK IT FROM YOUR BEST CRYSTAL FLUTES. BUT IF YOU CADGED A BOTTLE OF MIDDLING CHAMPAGNE FROM YOUR LAST OFFICE PARTY, YOU WOULD BE BEST TO SAVE IT FOR A MIMOSA AT BRUNCH.

INGREDIENTS
1 BOTTLE SPARKLING WINE, CAVA, PROSECCO OR CHAMPAGNE
1 CARTON ORANGE JUICE
TRIPLE SEC
STRAWBERRY (OPTIONAL)

PREPARATION
FILL HALF OF A CHAMPAGNE FLUTE WITH CHAMPAGNE. TOP OFF WITH CHILLED ORANGE JUICE. ADD JUST A SPLASH OF TRIPLE SEC. GENTLY STIR. GARNISH WITH A SLICE OF STRAWBERRY (OPTIONAL).

ALWAYS COOK WITH LIQUOR THAT YOU WOULD
ENJOY DRINKING ON ITS OWN. AFTER ALL, YOU WILL
BE COOKING OFF ALL THE ALCOHOLIC CONTENT,
AND ALL YOU REALLY HAVE LEFT IS THE TASTE.

One of the finest things that one can do with alcohol is to cook with it. Just a single bottle of wine in the cupboard can enable the least experienced chef to whip up a reputable beef bourguignon, cioppino, *coq a vin*, Korean BBQ, chicken cordon bleu, beef stroganoff, or kung pao chicken. With a fully stocked liquor cabinet the options are staggering and mouth watering: *penne a la vodka*, beer battered fish and chips, chicken marsala, bananas foster, tequila marinated hanger steak, duckling *a la orange*, and port wine poached pears can all be on the menu. ■ It's surprising how much great street food is also enhanced by a dash of liquor. My local roach coach serves world class tequila-marinated shrimp tacos on Fridays. All over Paris there are little carts designed to provide you with the instant gratification of a Grand Marnier crepe. And in Britain you can get a BrewBurger that has an aged beef patty,

Comte cheese and bacon candied with BrewDog's iconic amber ale. What's not to love? ■ Two last thoughts about alcohol and food. First, if you cook with bad wine, you will get bad bourguignon. Always cook with liquor that you would enjoy drinking on its own. After all, you will be cooking off all the alcoholic content, and all you really have left is the taste. Second, almost everything tastes better with a splash of booze. You can prove that by trying my mother in law's barbecue sauce recipe.

TENNESSEE WHISKEY BBQ SAUCE

INGREDIENTS
1 TABLESPOON CANOLA OIL
1/4 CUP ONION, FINELY MINCED
1/2 CUP WHISKEY (USE THE GOOD STUFF)
2/3 CUP KETCHUP
1/2 CUP CIDER VINEGAR
1 TEASPOON WORCESTERSHIRE SAUCE
1 TABLESPOON TABASCO
A FEW DROPS OF LIQUID SMOKE

PREPARATION
HEAT THE CANOLA OIL IN A MEDIUM SAUCEPAN OVER MEDIUM HEAT. ADD ONION AND SAUTE. DEGLAZE PAN WITH WHISKEY. ADD THE REST OF THE INGREDIENTS AND WHISK TOGETHER. BRING TO A SIMMER. REDUCE HEAT TO LOW AND COOK FOR 20 MINUTES. REMOVE FROM HEAT.

B
U
D
W
E
I
S
E
R

BUDWEISER, THE
KING OF BEERS, WAS
INTRODUCED TO THE
UNITED STATES IN 1876
BY ADOLPHUS BUSCH,
AND IT BILLS ITSELF AS
AN "ICON OF AMERICAN
VALUES LIKE OPTIMISM
AND CELEBRATION."

In 2012 I embarked on a great American road trip on the Blues Highway, which runs from New Orleans to Chicago. It was my first time in what we native Californians like to call the fly-over states, and I began to understand, somewhere around Mississippi, why I was always surprised at the outcome of national elections. It turns out that I had never truly lived in the actual United States. The real United States is Budweiser country and its epicenter, figuratively and literally, is the Budweiser Brewery in St. Louis, Missouri. ■ Budweiser, the King of Beers, was introduced to the United States in 1876 by Adolphus Busch, and it bills itself as an "icon of American values like optimism and celebration." I suppose that is a loose translation of the famous lines in the Declaration of Independence. Budweiser sponsors all things manly and patriotic, including Nascar and the NFL. Everyone knows that most people who watch the Superbowl are actually just waiting for the Budweiser halftime commercials — and the wait is usually worth it. How about that little Labrador puppy who fell in love with one of the Budweiser Clydesdales? Now that's America for you. ■ Sporting a red, white and blue label, complete with eagles rampant, the Budweiser logo is a staple feature of sporting arenas all over the United States, and while the craft beer movement has cut into corporate profits a bit in the 21st century, no one is expecting Mirror Lake, Moose Drool, or Anchor Steam to be sponsoring the American World Cup Soccer team anytime soon. That is undisputed Budweiser territory. ■ For 133 years, Budweiser's medium-bodied, crisp, American-style lager has been America's draft of choice, and I have the baseball cap to prove it. When in Saudi Arabia, wear a chador; when in the heartland, wear a Budweiser Black Crown Amber t-shirt.

BUDWEISER

WHILE THERE ARE MANY BEER COCKTAILS, MOST OF THE GOOD ONES, LIKE A BLACK AND TAN, INVOLVE UNPATRIOTIC ALES LIKE IRELAND'S GUINNESS. SO JUST GRAB A COLD ONE FROM THE FRIDGE, AND POP THE TOP, BECAUSE THIS BUD'S FOR YOU MR. AMERICA.

FROM CARUSO TO BOB DYLAN, SARAH BERNHARDT TO
GEORGE CLOONEY, LILLIE LANGTRY TO COCO CHANEL,
EVERYONE WHO WAS ANYONE HAS GONE THERE TO SAMPLE
HARRY CRADDOCK'S FAMOUS WHITE LADY COCKTAIL,
WITH ITS PLYMOUTH GIN AND FROTHY EGG WHITE.

There are hundreds of bars around the world that are as famous for their renowned customers as for their savory drinks, and I have been on a mission to visit all of them. I started this project many years ago in Venice, where I had my first Bellini at Harry's Bar, and tried to imagine where Orson Welles, Truman Capote and Peggy Guggenheim sat when they drank Giuseppe Cipriani's signature drink, a charming concoction of peach puree and Prosecco. Eventually, I preferred to share my cocktails with the ghosts of Dickens, Proust and Lord Byron at Caffe Florian, the first café in Venice that allowed women to enter. ■ In Paris of course I hit the Deux Margot, and tried not to think of how shabbily Jean-Paul Sartre treated Simone de Beauvoir in front of Camus, Picasso and Brecht. In Dublin, it was straight to Davy Byrne's Pub, where Leopold Bloom in *Ulysses* stops for a gorgonzola cheese sandwich and a glass of burgundy. And no trip to New York is complete without paying homage to the "Vicious Circle" at the Algonquin Hotel, and imagining Dorothy Parker holding forth at the Round Table. Chasing down Hemingway in Key West was a little trickier, as both Sloppy Joe's and Captain Tony's Saloon claim his exclusive patronage, so I figured, I might as well visit both, and order a greyhound at one and a dacquiri at the other — settling the other great Hemingway conundrum — which was Papa's favorite drink? ■ But the bar I always longed to visit was The American Bar at the Savoy in London, which is universally acknowledged as the pre-eminent watering hole for the rich and famous for the last two centuries. From Caruso to Bob Dylan, Sarah Bernhardt to George Clooney, Lillie Langtry to Coco Chanel, everyone who was anyone has gone there to sample Harry Craddock's famous White Lady cocktail, with its Plymouth gin and frothy egg white. So naturally, one balmy night, after the theatre, feeling wildly civilized, I walked across the Waterloo Bridge to have a nightcap and bask in reveries of George Bernard Shaw and Marlene Dietrich. Much to my dismay, the black jeans and dashing blue linen blazer that had served me so well in China, got me barred from the Savoy. No denim allowed. What could I do but tell them that I love a bar with standards and return the next night properly attired to cavort with the likes of Elizabeth Taylor and Sophia Loren?

WHITE LADY

INGREDIENTS
2 OZ GIN (PLYMOUTH)
1/2 OZ COINTREAU
1/2 OZ FRESH LEMON JUICE
1 FRESH EGG WHITE

PREPARATION
ADD ALL THE INGREDIENTS INTO A SHAKER AND FILL WITH ICE. SHAKE.
STRAIN INTO A CHILLED COCKTAIL GLASS.

MY COMPANION CAUGHT THE EYE OF THE HANDSOME BANDLEADER, AND A COUPLE OF MARGARITAS AND A FEW MORE COWBOYS FURTHER INTO THE EVENING, IT SEEMED LIKE A GOOD IDEA TO SWITCH TO TEQUILA SHOTS.

Durango, Colorado was named after Durango, Mexico and though it is far north of the border towns (Tijuana, Ensenada, Jerez) where the margarita is thought to have originated, it is still a margarita hot spot. Folks regularly line up at the bar of the Strater Hotel for a Belle Diamond Margarita, kick back in their Dan Post boots, and sing along to the ragtime music that inspired the best novels of Louis L'Amour. ■ Speaking of amour. Because my best friend is cuter than a basset hound tripping on its own ears, we received more than our fair share of male attention and free drinks. I even became rather fond of a young man we called Missouri, until I told him my age, and he recoiled in disbelief and stammered, "you're old enough to be my mother." I assured him that I'd never been in Durango before, and oddly enough that seemed to make everything all right. My companion caught the eye of the handsome bandleader, and a couple of margaritas and a few more cowboys further into the evening, it seemed like a good idea to switch to tequila shots. ■ Since this was a first for my friend, I had to show her how to breathe out, lick (the salt), down (the tequila) and bite (the lime). She followed my instructions exactly… even using my hand for the shooter ritual. It occurred to me briefly that this little oversight might cost us our lives in this aggressively masculine environment, but much to my surprise, the boys in the Stetsons just lined up the Hornitos shots in front of us and begged us over and over to "do that again." I got a new appreciation in the Belle Diamond Saloon for Joe Nichols' song, "Tequila Makes Her Clothes Fall Off."

MARGARITA

INGREDIENTS
1 1/2 OZS TEQUILA (HORNITOS AT THE SLATER)
1/2 OZ TRIPLE SEC
1 OZ FRESH LIME JUICE
LIME WEDGE
SALT OR SUGAR TO RIM THE GLASS (OPTIONAL)

PREPARATION
POUR THE INGREDIENTS INTO A COCKTAIL SHAKER WITH ICE CUBES. SHAKE WELL. IF DESIRED, SALT THE RIM OF A CHILLED MARGARITA GLASS. POUR CONTENTS, WITH ICE, INTO THE GLASS. GARNISH WITH THE LIME WEDGE.

IN A WELL DESIGNED TASTING GLASS, EVEN SOMEONE WITH BRONCHITIS CAN TELL THAT TALISKER 10 YEAR OLD SCOTCH IS HEAVY WITH PEAT SMOKE AND HAS JUST A HINT OF SALT AIR, WHILE GLENLIVET 12 YEAR OLD WHISKEY IS ALL VANILLA, HONEY AND PRESSED APPLES.

Not many years ago, I had a very intractable case of bronchitis that required sequential runs of the antibiotic Zithromax and abstinence from alcohol. The shame was that my appetite for food and drink was unimpaired, and so I dearly missed my filet mignons and my occasional hot toddies. Eventually, a good friend, who is a master blender, pointed out to me that you don't have to drink the stuff to enjoy it. And that began my real appreciation for the aroma of certain fine liquors. ■ During my recovery, instead of tastings, we staged several nosings. We would line up six or seven vodkas, rums or whiskeys and spend a good deal of time trying to describe what we were smelling. While there are really only five basic flavors, there are literally tens of thousands of individual scents, and unfortunately only a handful of words in the English language to describe them. For example, just take a moment to try and describe how an avocado smells. ■ That is why, when nosing, it's important to have the right glass for the right liquor. The shape of

the correct glass insures that the aroma reaches
your olfactory glands in just the right way to
be fully appreciated and perhaps described.
In a well designed tasting glass, even someone
with bronchitis can tell that Talisker 10 year old
Scotch is heavy with peat smoke and has just
a hint of salt air, while Glenlivet 12 year old
whiskey is all vanilla, honey and pressed apples.

TASTING/ NOSING GLASSES

ONLY RECENTLY, GLENCAIRN CRYSTAL REALIZED THAT
WHISKEY NEEDED ITS OWN SPECIAL GLASS, JUST LIKE CHAM-
PAGNE OR BRANDY, SO THAT THE TRUE FLAVORS AND AROMAS
OF THE MORE REFINED SINGLE MALTS COULD BE FULLY
APPRECIATED. SO IF WHISKEY NOSING APPEALS TO YOU, THIS
IS WHERE YOU CAN FIND THE PERFECT TASTING/NOSING
GLASS: WWW.WHISKYGLASS.COM.

It's hard to remember back to a time when only the wines of France were taken seriously, and one had to travel to Johannisberg Schloss in Rheingau to taste a really first rate Spätlese. Italian wines were for starving students, or in my father's mind, cranky babies, and the wines of the rest of the world were not even on the oenophile's map. ■ Back in the day, there was a struggling wine area in California called Napa Valley, anchored by the old wineries of the monks at Christian Brothers and the newer family owned vineyards at Mondavi and Sutter Home. In the 60's, one could drive California Highway 19 on a weekday and never see another fellow traveller in any of the free tasting rooms. Now one has to rent a limo to navigate the congested roads and insure that one won't end up with a fresh DUI to go with that spectacular Cabernet bought at the $25 tasting room at Beringer. ■ As you can see, it is tempting at the end of this little book of reminiscences to indulge in a fit of nostalgia. Oh, the good old days: sipping a Dubonnet at what one used to call dinner parties; drinking an Irish Coffee at the Buena Vista in San Francisco, where the drink was invented; discovering Galliano and the inimitable Harvey Wallbanger on an Amtrak excursion; encountering 100+ artisanal tequilas at Marias in Santa Fe. ■ But I intend on having some amazing memories twenty years from now, so I am counting on the best drink or cocktail I have ever had to be the one I drink tonight. I'm going to continue to scour the local BevMo for a bitters I have never tasted. Stop in at the local hot spot and see what my indigenous mixologists are up to. Splurge on that really great bottle of champage on my next cruise. Take a vintage port to bed. ■ Cheers! Gan bei! Prost! Cin cin. Kampai! Skål! Salud!

Cheers!

CPSIA information can be obtained at www.ICGtesting.com
Printed in the USA
BVOW11*2046191214

380099BV00011B/24/P